Freaking Idiot's Guide to Fiverr

How people are making $1000 a month providing simple services

By Nick Vulich
Copyright 2013

Thank you for purchasing this book. **Freaking Idiot's Guide to Making Money with Fiverr** is an attempt to bring you easy to implement solutions for selling your services on Fiverr. While no book can guarantee you success, the author and publisher have made every attempt to bring you the latest information that has been found to work for other Fiverr sellers. Results can vary.

If you find the contents helpful, please consider taking a few moments to leave a review on Amazon.

Your comments will help other readers decide if this book may be useful to them in their journey to be a Fiverr seller. They will also help me to catch errors or omissions in this book, and to correct them as quickly as possible.

If you have any comments or questions, feel free to contact me at nick@digitalhistoryproject.com. Any corrections will be addressed in future editions.

Table of Contents

In the beginning ...

Fiverr is a freelance website where sellers list a gig (any service – crazy ass or otherwise) that they are willing to provide for five bucks!

The cool part is, everything on Fiverr is priced at $5.00, not a penny more, or less – MAYBE! (but we'll get to that part a little later). I know what you're thinking – Five bucks! That's crazy! Who's going to do anything for five bucks anymore? But, you'd be surprised.

When the time came for me to purchase my first Kindle book cover, I couldn't afford to pay $300 to $500 for a professional graphic designer, so I figured what the hell? I dropped five bucks on a Fiverr.

Now I'm a serial Fiverr!

That five bucks led to me spending $190 in my first 20 days on the site. It's addictive. It's fun. And, it's just crazy what all of these people are willing to do for only five bucks.

***

Here are just a few things you might not know about Fiverr.

1) Fiverr was launched in February 2010.
2) It was founded by Micha Kaufman and Shai Wininger.
3) All gigs are priced at $5.00.
4) Sellers receive $3.93 for each completed gig (Fiverr's take is $1.00, and PayPal fees grab another 8 cents).

5) As of January 2013, there are over 1,000,000 gigs listed on Fiverr.

6) According to Alexa, Fiverr is ranked the top 195th site in the world, and 185th in the United States.

7) In 2011 and 2012 alone, Fiverr received over $20 million in venture capital financing

8) Every gig on Fiverr starts out with the words "I will [fill in the blank] for $5.00."

What can you sell on Fiverr?

What can you sell on Fiverr?

Perhaps a better question is, what can't you sell on Fiverr? A quick look at the website shows people offering a number of normal and not so normal services.

Before we even try to pin down any ideas for what you should sell, let's take a look at some of the crazy ass shit on Fiverr that is selling well.

1) There's this middle aged dude (anibalf). His offer is to sing a depressing Happy Birthday as a mouse. In what you can see of his cover video there's an old dude wearing a Mickey Mouse hat and he really does seem to be depressed. Any guesses how many of these he's sold over the last year? 107! That's 107 people shelling out five bucks each to see a depressing old man sing the Happy Birthday song in a Mickey Mouse Hat.

2) Jebediahjenkins will do anything you want (within reason) as a redneck for $5.00. His cover photo shows this redneck geek in a cowboy hat in front of a confederate flag. He can sing, play his "geetar," and even deliver a special "redneck-ified" message. For $10.00 more he will do it outdoors, and for $20.00 he will rush deliver this video extravaganza in only two days instead of the normal five. And, in case you were wondering, he's sold 67 gigs in the last seven months.

3) And, there is this girl – (ragcloll). She will "write your name, link or any words" on her "sexy butt." Get this – You even get to choose the color of her sexy thong (for a $20.00 gig extra). Add another $20.00, and she will have her friend join her for two sexy butt messages. She's sold 35 gigs in less than four months. She also offers a similar "boob" gig that shows 67 sales in the last five months.

4) (Extrainput) offers to "distribute 30 flyers in New York City or around Baruch College." He has numerous gig extras, and offers photo proof that the job is actually done. A few of the gig extras include: Print and handout 100 color flyers $20.00, move it up to 300 flyers for $50.00. Business appears to be booming as he has delivered on 592 gigs in six months. I've seen two other guys offering similar services in Chicago and Philadelphia. Both of them have collected over 150 gigs.

5) This one may top them all for sheer craziness. (mdlasky) offers to "record an Xmas greeting or anything else as Jesus." The man has some really crazy pictures to enhance the listing. He has sold 682 gigs in the last year. And, yes – he will graciously accept tips for Jesus in his "tip jar."

6) This one hasn't gotten many takers, but maybe it will help you come up with some ideas. (madame_marie) offers to cast a psychic spell "giving you bigger boobs." Perhaps we can find one like this for guys, but aimed a little lower?

7) (drewapple) will "draw you a penis for $5.00." The offer is to draw you a "cute or funny or ugly or scary or kawaii or realistic or fantastic penis." Some of them even have faces or beards. Not a big mover yet, but it's only been a gig for two weeks.

8) Perhaps a professional video testimonial is more to your liking. (Screamingfinger) has collected 1111 gigs in the last year for his offer to "give you a video testimonial with/out business suit." He offers five gig extras for from $10.00 to $40.00. (Banjoman15) has a similar offer to "give a real looking testimonial" for which he has collected 744 gigs. He can also promote your product as Albert Einstein.

9) Everyone dreams about being rich someday. This offer from (nogalicious) is to meditate on your "financial abundance for five minutes straight." According to the gig details page "windfalls are not uncommon," and she invites tips based upon your good fortune – a "3% to 10% tip" to be exact. I'd laugh, but she's collected 291 gigs on this one in the last two years. Another gig from this woman will help you get pregnant. And, just in case you still have a problem, she has a gig extra on this one offering her top five fertility tips for only $5.00.

Are you beginning to get the idea? There is no limit to the type of gig that you can offer. If you can imagine it, you can do it.

Getting started

It really can't get any simpler than this.

Go to Fiverr.com. Select join at the top of the page. That will take you to the sign-up screen. Once there you have the option to Join with Facebook, or to sign-up using your email address.

The toughest choice you will have to make is selecting your user name. I suggest you give this a little thought. Your user name is how people are going to get to know you on Fiverr. SexyGrandma or CowboyDan are cool names, but if your intention is to make money, neither of those names is probably going to help you very much.

An effective username should tell people something about you. A good example here is one of Fiverr's hottest celebrities – Professor Puppet. Right away, without knowing anymore about him, you can guess that he does something related to puppets. If you plan on purchasing a custom logo design - Would you rather order from foxontherun or logomaster? Logomaster screams out what you do, and sort of sets you up as an expert at it in people's minds. Same thing if you are offering blog writing services, would you prefer katesservices or seowriterkate?

One other way to go with it is to just use your name – johnqpublic. Think about it for a minute. 99 percent of all sellers are going to have a made up name, but you had the guts (or lack of creativity) to use your own name. It may be the extra boost you need to instill confidence in your abilities.

Writing your first Fiverr Description page

Fiverr has a very simple to understand form for inputting your gig information. To access it click on the **seller** button at the top of the page, and from the drop down menu select **create a new gig**.

That will bring up the gig entry form.

Here's a simple explanation of how to fill out this form.

I will [   ] for $5.00. Type in your offer. Tell the world what you are willing to do for $5.00.

Category. Click on the category and subcategory buttons, and select the category that best describes your listing.

Description. Fiverr gives you 1200 characters to write your description. Try to use as much of it as you can, sprinkling keywords in where appropriate.

Instructions to Buyer. These are the instructions that will be sent to sellers when they purchase your gig. Clearly state what your buyer needs to provide for you to get to work on their project.

Tags. Include as many relevant tags as possible. This will increase traffic to your gig.

Maximum Days to Complete. State how long it will take you to deliver your gig. Allow enough time – you don't want to deliver late.

Add Image. Submit your gig pictures or videos. Optimum picture size is 265 pixels high x 380 pixels wide.

This Item Requires Shipping. Click this box if you have a physical item to mail.

Click save when finished.

***

That's it. Your gig is live, and you are open for business on Fiverr.

Don't worry if you're not sure how to fill everything out yet. The next section is going to cover the same information, but we will approach it in more detail, and based upon what the buyer sees.

Your Offer

Every gig on Fiverr starts with the statement "I will [fill in the blank] for $5.00."

One offer from Professor Puppet says, "I will record a custom video about anything you like for $5.00."

It is simple, straightforward, and tells exactly what he is offering to do. It has the keywords "record" and "custom video." The gig header also shows that he listed it in the category, *video and animation / puppet*. And, to build confidence in the seller, it shows that this gig was created "almost 2 years ago." One suggestion would be to add the word "puppet." Right now it won't show up at all for people specifically looking for a puppet video.

When anyone types either of these two keywords into Fiverr's search engine its spiders start going out through the site looking for matches. Now no one can tell you for sure just how Fiverr decides how to display the listings it returns. Obviously they look for the best keyword matches, and probably a combination of how many gigs the seller has collected and how long the gig has been running. One other thing I have noticed is, if there are any *top rated sellers* in the category, either one or two of them will normally get the first and second slots in the list of items displayed.

Another listing from McCold offers to "…create [a] killer Blackboard or Whiteboard promotional animated video for $5.00."

The seller has three strong keywords – "blackboard," "whiteboard," and "animated video." These are the keywords Fiverr and Google will pick up when anyone is searching for them. The gig is listed in the category *video & animation / commercials*, and it was created 2 months ago.

The seller also adds the word "killer" to describe his service. On any other site I would say there's no need for it. No one is going to type "killer" in the search box when they're looking for an animated video. Fiverr is different, though. Over a third of its sellers include at least one adjective in their descriptions and it does seem to make the description stand out more.

Some of the adjectives you're going to see bantered around Fiverr include:

1) Killer
2) Fantastic
3) Awesome
4) High Quality
5) Attractive
6) Unique
7) Cool
8) Stunning
9) Professional

All I can say is try it for yourself, and see which one works best for you. Make one gig listing with an adjective or two thrown in, and another without.

Information Box

The information box gives you basic information about the seller, and the gig.

In the information box for Professor Puppet you can see the following information:

1) Sellers name, and cover picture
2) Flag showing the country the seller is from
3) Estimated delivery time if you order the gig
4) Gig rating expressed as a percentage. A quick way to check how happy people are with the sellers offering.
5) How many orders are in the order queue. This shows you how many orders the seller has to do before he gets to yours. Buyers can use this to decide if you want to use the gig extra for faster turnaround.
6) Seller rating. Level One, Level Two, or Top Rated Seller.

Killerlogo2013's info box shows you how fast things can get rolling on Fiverr if you have the right offer. In this case, the offer has been running for one day. The seller has absolutely no rating on Fiverr – no reputation at all. Despite all of that he has 17 orders in his queue in just one day.

Your goal is to make this box as impressive as all hell. The better it looks the more gigs you will have in your queue.

Gig Pictures

The more examples of your work that you can show to people, the more sales you are going to make. The reason for this is: people are going to look through your portfolio for ideas, and when they see something they like, they're going to start to picture it as their own. Think about it for a minute. The same thing happens when you go searching for a new car. When you see one you like, you begin forming a mental picture of yourself driving it, only maybe in a different color, or with the fancy stereo system and heated leather seats. That's what you want to make potential customers do when they see your offer. If you can make them start visualizing how your service will look or work for them, you've got the sale.

With that said, what can you do to make sure you have the most effective cover image possible?

A quick check of Fiverr will show three leading styles of images being used by most sellers: a short video (30 seconds is the max allowed) outlining the services you offer, or your best sample of a video that you made for a customer - a picture of your work – or a picture of yourself.

The least you should know about pictures.

1) Optimal picture size is 265 pixels high x 380 pixels wide.
2) Fiver allows you to upload multiple picture files.

3) Your gig pictures are displayed in a carousel underneath your item description and rotate around. An arrow also pops up at the edges of your pictures so clients can scroll forward or backward through your samples.

There's no right or wrong answer here about which style of cover image to go with. You should probably let your offering help you make the decision. If you're gig is for a custom video, you probably want to lead with samples of the types of videos you make. A selection of fifteen of twenty videos from your portfolio will give potential customers a good way to sample what you can do for them.

Professor Puppet offers a good example of using videos for your cover image.

There is a really nicely framed image of his puppet, Professor Hans Von Puppet. And, there is a large carousel of sample videos (located under the main video) for potential clients to view. You should also check out the lighting in his picture – It's perfect. There are no shadows or dark spots anywhere. Make that your goal with every picture you post.

Another seller ragcloll uses pictures very effectively to highlight her offer.

She has a collage with pictures of women's butts clad in sexy bikini bottoms. Written across each bum is a sample of the type of messages she can add. Did I mention she sells pictures with your message written on her butt or boobs!

Who says sex doesn't sell?

With the right product a collage of pictures can make your offer stand out from the crowd. The photography ragcloll uses is professional grade. It is close up, and in your face. The images are clear, without shadows or dark spots. And, in this case she chose to put a border around each of the smaller pictures which makes them stand out even more.

Final word of advice, don't be stingy with your pictures. Post enough of them so potential buyers can really get the flavor for your idea, and be comfortable that they understand how your offering can help them solve their problems.

The final style is to put a big picture of yourself out there. Often times, just being able to see a picture of who they are dealing with can give customers a warm and fuzzy feeling about you, if you chose the right picture, that is! If you decide this is the way you want to go, make sure the picture you use is appropriate to what you are selling. The first thing that you need to do is paste a big smile across your face. If your offering is business related, formal dress should be the rule. Guys that means white shirt and tie, possibly even a suit coat. Gals, you should go for a dress or appropriate business attire. If your offer is artsy, go for whatever you think is best, just not too far out there – you don't want to scare people away.

One last SEO trick to drive more traffic to your gigs - always label your pictures with a combination of keywords related to your gig. I know it's a hell of a lot easier to just name your pictures gig 1, gig 2, gig 3, and so on. But one thing I've learned from blogging, and selling on eBay – Google loves pictures. If you need proof, Google anything you can think of, and most of the time they will bring up a gallery of pictures labeled "images for [your search term]." Google gathers these pictures from all over the web, and displays them whenever anyone searches for a similar topic.

And, yes, people do click on those images, over and over again.

Writing out the offer details

Most sellers only do an adequate job of describing their gig.

Your goal is to bump your description up a notch or two. You want to clearly and concisely layout the details of your gig. Be sure to tell people exactly what you can and cannot do. The rule is, if there's any doubt, spell it out. The last thing that you want to do is get bad feedback over a simple misunderstanding. Also, be sure to say what you won't do, "Sorry no porn, violence, or hate sites." It's ok to layout ground rules.

Start out with a brief description of your offer.

> "I will custom design your logo, with two revisions at no additional charge."
> "I will create a 30 second testimonial or review for your product using my spokes-puppet, Dr. Bob the Blob."
> "Best artwork offered on Fiverr. I will custom draw you as a zombie."
> "Post your logo, URL, or custom words on my sexy butt. I guarantee it will draw second looks."

After you are finished with this brief description, you can go into more details. And explain what your offer is all about, and how you operate.

Check out this description from shiftypop.

She gives just enough information about herself, and her previous work. She goes on to mention the equipment she has available to record your jingle, and admonishes that "you'd be silly to miss out on this gig!"

It's a great sales pitch! It tells you exactly what you get – "a 30 second instrumental for $5." And, she invites you to message her with questions.

Overall, it's a great gig description.

Other sellers lead with their stats, attempting to build confidence in their offering. Read this one over:

Level two seller on Fiverr. 1250+ gigs done! 100% rating. I am a Photoshop expert. I will create an awesome logo for your business. I guarantee that you will be 100% satisfied. Test me for only $5.00. You give me your company name, color choice and some suggestions. Or, let me just work my magic.

After they have established their authority, they go into their offer, description, and sales pitch.

Add tags to help your gig get found

Tags are nothing more than a selection of keywords that you can add to your gig to help it get noticed by Fiverr and Google when people search for the services that you offer.

You want to start out with the obvious ones first. If you're selling logo design you can start out with – logos, logo design, graphic design, business services, company branding. You also want to throw in a few other keywords that are not quite related to what you sell, but where your service could be used with it. In the case of logo design, we could also add stationary design, letterhead design, website banners and headers, and Facebook and Twitter branding. People who use these services also need a logo, so you could pick up some extra business using these tags.

If you're not sure how to tag your gig, type your gig name into the Fiverr search bar. That should give you two or three other terms from the drop down menu. Another good way to find keywords is to look through the gig descriptions written by top sellers and level two sellers. As you look through the listings, write down any keywords you come across.

At this point you should have at least ten or twelve good keywords. If you want to research them a little further you can visit the Google Keyword Tool. Using it you can type in your keywords and Google will tell you how many searches are made for that particular keyword, and suggest similar keywords that you may want to explore.

When you are happy with what you have enter them in the "tags" section of the Fiverr listing form.

Gig extras are where the money is at

To add gig extras to your listing you need to be a Level One Seller. That means that you need to have completed 10 gigs in the previous thirty days with at least a 90 percent feedback rating.

When you hit level one you will receive an email from Fiverr notifying you. At the same time your gigs should automatically add the option for gig extras.

As a Level One Seller you can add three gig extras, plus extra fast delivery if you check the box at the bottom of the form. You can price each gig extra anywhere between $5.00 and $50.00.

If you're serious about making money on Fiverr you should add all of the extras you can to every gig. Many sellers have reported doubling or even tripling their income since the addition of gig extras.

According to sellers in the know you want to carefully pick your gig extras. The key to making real money is to offer extras that enhance your offering, but take little or no extra time to create. An example would be if you were designing custom artwork, you can offer to include a PSD file (that allows buyers to make their own corrections or updates) for $10.00 or $20.00. You already made the file when you did the work. The only thing you need to do extra is upload the PSD file with your order. Many sellers offering website design are adding a link to their webpage on every website they design. And, coincidentally one of their gig extras (you guessed it – for $10.00 or $20.00) is removing that link.

Smart sellers are designing their gigs around the types of gig extras they can offer. You should too. In the gig examples section later in this book, I offer a list of gig extras for every service to help get your creative juices flowing.

What About tips?

What if your work was so awesome? And, you delivered the goods three days early, after multiple revisions, and extras? Wouldn't it be great if your customers could show their eternal gratitude to you?

What if you asked them?

That's what many sellers are doing. Now they're not coming out and screaming "Give me a tip." What they are doing is offering a number of subtle hints, and some others that are not so subtle. My favorite is the "tip jar." It is showing up in more and more listings. A recent search showed lots of "tip jars" on Fiverr (actually I got tired of counting after 138).

Here is one example of the many "tip jars" you will find on Fiverr.

It's a pleasure and joy to work with great and generous clients like you. If I think I over delivered or that I deserve to be paid more, you can leave me a tip. Thank you for all the tips, they will help me to concentrate more on work and to develop my knowledge even further.

One thing I've noticed about the "tip jar" is – You need to take a moment to tell customers how great they are, and that you'd really appreciate any extra "love" that they will throw out there for you.

What if Five Dollars isn't a big enough tip? Your work was really awesome, wasn't it? How do you get customers to up their generosity a little without resorting to strong-arm tactics? Many sellers are putting their own spin on the "tip jar" by adding gig extras to it.

One seller gives some concrete examples of what he can do with various tips … $5.00 for hardware upgrades, $10.00 for a dog chewy, and $20.00 for dinner with the wifey. A few bold sellers are upping the ante even further, asking $50.00 and $100.00 for a tip. I'm not saying it will work every time, but what if even one in ten customers make the jump from $5.00 to $10.00 or $20.00. Life would be so much better, wouldn't it?

And, if you're a little uncomfortable about adding a "tip jar," do what other sellers are doing – add a disclosure. Many of the "tip jar" descriptions I've seen say they only offer it because they have received customer complaints that they didn't have a "tip jar." Sorry, not my fault. It's here because my customers demanded I have one.

What's all of this talk about levels

Fiverr has developed a rating system for their sellers separating them into three different levels based upon the number of gigs they have completed and how well they take care of their customers

The levels are:

Level One -.

Requirements

1) Need to be a member for 30 days.

2) Complete 10 gigs in the past 30 days with a minimum feedback rating of 90%.

Benefits

Gig extras open up giving sellers the opportunity to significantly increase income.

Level Two

Requirements

1) Complete over 50 gigs in the past 60 days

2) Feedback rating of 90% or better.

Benefits

Upon reaching level two more sales tools are unlocked for sellers. Another key advantage is, buyers are allowed to purchase up to eight of a single gig, allowing you to further increase your income.

Top Rated Seller

Requirements

Becoming a Top Rated Seller is a lot like rushing an exclusive fraternity. According to the Fiverr Blog Top Rated Sellers are "mutually" chosen by the editors of Fiverr. During this hush-hush process some of the factors considered are seniority, sales volume, and "extremely high" customer feedback. Don't overlook sending flowers or chocolates – especially if you start thinking you may be close to being chosen.

Benefits

Top Rated Sellers get even more advanced selling tools, plus access to beta features and VIP support. Another major benefit is you can charge up to $100.00 for gig extras.

Getting Paid

You've done all your work, and delivered gig after gig on time, now comes the big question – How do you get paid?

The first thing you need to know is Fiverr makes all payments through PayPal, so if you haven't done it yet, you need to link your PayPal account to your Fiverr account.

Just so you know Fiverr starts working on paying you as soon as you deliver your gig. After waiting for the buyer to accept your gig, it normally takes 14 to 17 days to process your payment.

You can check the payments you have coming anytime by visiting **Mission Control** in your **Payments Center**.

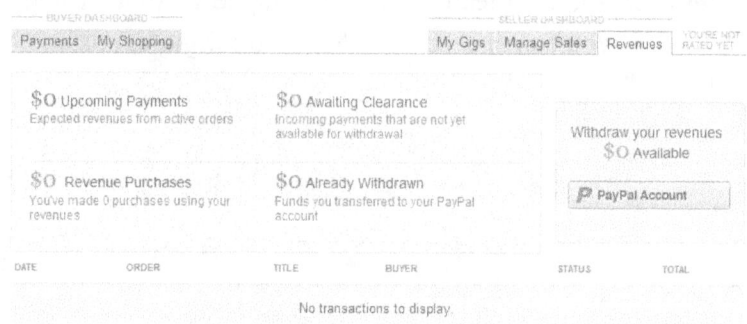

Mission Control is simple to understand after you've given it a once over.

Upcoming Payments is the money you will be receiving once you deliver all of those gigs that are currently waiting in your queue.

Awaiting Clearance is money that is on its way to you, but still on hold in Fiverr's 14 day waiting system.

Revenue Purchases are just that, any purchases that you made on Fiverr using your account balance.

Already Withdrawn shows the amount you have already transferred to your PayPal account.

The smaller blue box to the right of the bigger one is the most important. It shows the amount of money you actually have available to transfer to your PayPal account. When you're ready to collect your cash, just click on the **PayPal Account** button.

***

A note on payments: Customers pay $5.00 for your basic gig. Of that $5.00 Fiverr keeps $1.00 (or 20%), the seller receives the other $4.00 less another 8 cents to PayPal for transaction fees. So your net earnings work out to about $3.92 per gig. The house take on gig extras and tips is the same – 20 %, so if you have a $20.00 gig extra, you net $16.00 (less another 32 cents to PayPal).

Hints on picking a profitable gig

One thing all sellers say is that when you pick a gig, you've really got to think things out if you want to make any money. According to John, in Iowa City, who has been selling on Fiverr for just over a year now – "You want to pick simple gigs that you can complete in five minutes, ten at the very most."

The real secret to making money on Fiverr is to find a popular gig that several successful Level 2 and Top Rated Sellers are doing, but put your own spin on it.

Jan, in Des Moines, suggests that "for your first ten or twenty gigs while you're trying two crack Level One, do whatever it takes. Offer some of the Top Rated Sellers gig extras for free. Whatever money you lose in the beginning, you're going to get twice as much back when you can start charging for those gig extras. The only thing you should be thinking about your first month is delivering every gig on time, and making your customers happy."

"Once you hit Level One," Jan says, "it's time to revisit those early gigs. Now you can add the gig extras, and take your business past the fiverr."

John did it different. "I added extra value to my gigs," he says. "But, I also wrote my own gig extras into the description. My first gig was selling SEO articles. My deal was for 250 words. I made sure to put right there in the gig – If you need it longer, no problem. For 400 words, order two gigs. For 600 words order three gigs. For 800 words order four gigs, and so on. I was getting gig extras from the start, just by suggesting they order extra gigs."

"Whatever services you offer," Jan adds, 'you really need to think beyond the five bucks. If you plan your gig right and add gig extras that add real value to your offer that five dollars is easily going to grow to $20.00, $30.00, many times even $50.00. And, even if you don't get any gig extras, a lot of people buy multiple gigs."

If you still need a little inspiration to figure out what gigs you want to offer be sure to check out the next section.

Twenty-Nine Gigs That Will Make You Money

Here is a list of twenty-nine gigs already doing well on Fiverr. Hopefully they will get your creative juices flowing, and help you decide on a few gigs to get your business started.

For each gig I have included a description of what it's all about, suggestions for gig extras that current sellers are offering, and a few links to sellers offering these services now. If you decide to offer similar gigs, visit the included links. Take a few minutes to study their offering. Read some of their reviews to see what customers liked about their services, or if there was something buyers wished would have been included or done differently. This will show you opportunities to improve on the current gigs being offered.

Whatever services you eventually chose to offer, be sure to put your own spin on them. Be creative, add humor if appropriate, and offer more than your competitors. Any extra work you put in will pay off in building positive feedback, gig extras, and more tips in your "tip jar." You did plan on having a really big tip jar – didn't you?

Job seeker services include writing resumes, cover letters, critiquing resumes and cover letters, and offering advice on interviewing skills. Overall it is a so-so category on Fiverr. I didn't come across any big time sellers. Many of the people selling these services have been doing it for one or two years, and have collected 50 to 100 gigs. Most of the gig descriptions are short with very few details. My suggestion would be to write a detailed description of your qualifications, how you have helped other people, and to offer lots of gig extras to upgrade your service.

1) **QR Resume**. Mobile is hot! More and more people, including busy hiring managers are conducting business with their phone. One way you can help job seekers is to provide a mobile web based resume with a QR code. Smart sellers are including job seeker photos, videos, a QR code, and free web hosting. Many sellers also include a link to their web page at the bottom to drive more sales.
>Gig extras: removing the link to your website, creating a personalized subdomain, and including the source code so buyers can build a regular website as well.
>Links: musiclover ashisharora

2) **Resume Writing.** Everyone needs a little help job hunting. If you have the ability to write effective copy, you can help job seekers with their resume. This could be a really sweet and easy gig if you set up ten or fifteen

different templates first. This way all you need to do is plug the information clients give you into the correct style of resume, and you're ready to go.

> Gig extras: create a customized cover letter, alter resume for a different career category, write and mail five resumes and cover letters.

> williams0789 mowche

3) **Interview Advice**. One guy seemed to be doing quite well at this. His offer was that he had talked to 25 top hiring managers collecting their advice on how to answer the top interview related questions. He has a really strong introductory video outlining his offer with a great call to action. Perhaps you could put a different spin on this by focusing on different industries – food service, management, sales, pharmaceuticals, you get the idea. You could easily post twenty gigs just on this. Your advice could be delivered on video, eBook, or a short printed list.

> Gig extras: offer top do's and don'ts list from an authority, provide a private consultation, Skype teleconference with customer, webinar on similar subject.

> Links: howtobecometv

Testimonials

Testimonials and reviews are a booming business on Fiverr. You name it – Anything from writing Kindle book reviews, website and movie reviews, business reviews, Facebook and YouTube likes. A lot of these people have racked up 1,000, 2,000, and even more of these gigs in less than one year.

After reading through these offerings, I'm not sure I would believe any business testimonial I come across. You have sweet old ladies, sexy young women, two high school girls, bald old men, rednecks, puppets, just about anything you can think off is offering to give you a review.

And, they come in all formats, too. Need streaming video, not a problem. Do you need a book review on Kindle or at Good Reads, at least twenty Fiverr's can do it for you. Is your Facebook page a little light on likes? There is no shortage of people willing and able to give you hundreds, even thousands of likes.

4) **Reviews for professional websites.** One woman's offer is to write a review on a professional realtor website. She can tailor the message to your needs or market, to help realtors build their brand, and increase trust and loyalty. This is another one of those that you can tailor for just about any business – car dealers, restaurants, banks, insurance companies, just about any type of salesmen.

Another idea would be to offer reviews on Yelp, Dealer Rater, Restaurants.com.

Gig extras: one day service, write two additional reviews, write four additional reviews.

Links: ac0704

5) **Video Review of Business.** Do you like performing on camera? Are you sincere and believable? This is a booming business. A lot of the video reviewers have collected thousands of gigs. You can do it too, if you can read a script, and look convincing on screen. The key here is to think of an angle, and promote the hell out of it. Are you an everyday guy? A retired senior? A college student or recent grad? You need to develop a persona that can cater to different market segments. Most of the offers are for a 30 second to two minute video. Sometimes the offer is to send you the video, other times it is to post the video on YouTube or a particular website.

Gig extras: record video in HD, upload video to YouTube or another website, 24 hour turnaround

Links: diariles sternfox stayingvintage (this girl collected 108 gigs in 2 months)

6) **Kindle book review**. It's a jungle out there. In the Amazon world you need reviews to sell books, and no one wants to be the first one to review a book. Because of this many authors are willing to pay for their first one or two reviews to get their book started. With this offer it is important to note that you will purchase the book, too. This is important because when you write a review after purchasing the book, it will be tagged as an Amazon

Verified Purchase, thus giving your review more credibility. Be sure to detail your review style. Will it be just a line or two? Will you offer a detailed review? Or, Will you pick out one or two points in the book to highlight? (Meowmeowkitty offers a different spin. She will write a negative review for someone's book. She's sold 27 gigs to date, so there must be a good deal of hating going on in the Kindle world).

Gig extras: most reviewers charge an extra gig if the book they are reviewing costs over 99 cents, if the book to reviewed costs over $2.99 they charge two extra gigs – 24 hour or 48 hour turnaround – like, or like an add tags for your book

Links: tylerjms7   meowmeowkitty   caspermerlin

Are you an experienced writer? Do you have experience writing in a particular field? Writing is an explosive growth market on Fiverr! It seems just about everyone is looking for someone to help them with blog posts, term papers, short articles, and even ghost writing services.

If you're really good, you can make a killing writing short 250 to 500 word articles. Many authors find people test them, asking them to create one or two articles for them. If they like what they see, you may end up writing ten to twenty articles a month for the same person.

The key here is not to overpromise, or you will end up overwhelmed with work. Set clear guidelines in your gig description. Tell people exactly what you will and will not do, how many words are included, if you will do research or if they need to provide information or an outline, and finally, be sure to set realistic guidelines. When you start out 24 hours may be an ok turnaround time, but when the gigs start pouring in, make sure you adjust your time frame accordingly.

7) **Website Bio**. Almost everyone can benefit from a great bio. Just a few of your potential prospects include: bloggers, businessmen, authors, students, job seekers, avid Facebookers. Every website you visit has a spot for a short biography. Let people know that you've got them covered. Offer to write an amazing bio tailored to the website they are going to post it on. Mention your credentials. Let

people know if you are a blogger, experienced web developer, or copywriter. Keep in mind most web bio's should be short (150 to 200 words) and concise, targeted to the type of visitors who visit that site.

Gig extras: offer to add multiple revisions, add hyperlinks or a picture, add content for additional pages on their website, 24 or 48 hour turnaround, write a longer bio

Links: amandaedwards nystrele

8) **Website Content.** Thousands of new blogs enter the blogosphere every day, and every one of them has the same need – new and unique content. If you can quickly research a topic, put a unique spin on the information you discover, and quickly churn out article after article that is informative and easy to read, this is definitely the gig for you. Make sure you carefully layout the ground rules for your offer. Tell everyone up front how many words you are offering to write, how much research you are willing and able to do, and how long it will take you to do it. If you need any information before you can start writing, let your buyer know. Most writers also state prohibitions up front. If don't want to write about pornography, violence, or hateful things, say it. It is ok to set boundaries and expectations. This is your business.

Gig Extras: increase the word count, additional research, source pictures or clipart, post to a website, quick turnaround, write in different language

Links: miacarter kevthefont choochypuss juanma28

9) **Edit documents for correct American Grammar.** Just about anywhere you turn on the web you see examples of

grammatical errors made by people not really familiar with English. This gig is an offer to correct those errors and make their text easier to read. If you can catch grammatical errors, and are able to properly reword sentences you can excel at this service. One seller has collected over 500 gigs in just one year.

Gig extras: longer texts, more difficult texts, scientific texts

Links: papina

10) **Proofread Documents**. This gig offers to proof read any essay, book, eBook, term paper for spelling and grammar. If you are familiar with proper English, syntax, and punctuation, this could be the gig for you. With more and more people running websites and writing eBooks there is a huge need and demand for professional proofreading. When you write your gig description, be sure to note any experience or education relevant to what you are doing.

Gig extras: longer documents, quick turnaround

Links: eboler abbiejoy21

11) **Email Marketing**. The goal of any email campaign is to get readers to click on your offer. To do that your copy has to be intriguing, and convincing. The truth is most marketers have no idea how to write an effective call to action. This is where you come in. If you can tempt and tantalize readers, and make them want to click on your offer, you will have a flood of repeat buyers.

Gig extras: write tantalizing subject lines, write a series of business oriented tweets, quick turnaround

Links: amyample

12) **Copyrighting**. Businesses turn to copyrighters when they need high impact marketing material. The idea is to present compelling copy that will turn readers into buyers. If you are experienced in advertising or marketing this could be a great gig for you. Offers start at Fiverrs's normal $5.00, but gig extras for longer assignment can easily bring your total take to $50.00 or $100.00. One seller I looked at had collected 279 gigs in the last five months, and had 18 orders in the queue. This gig is sizzling hot, if you can deliver the hot copy.

Gig extras: more words in 100 or 200 word increments, quicker turnaround

Links: grammargal brycetea

13) **Translation Services**. Are you fluent in a foreign language? This is another booming service on Fiverr. The typical offer is to translate 300 or 400 words, with additional words available as a gig upgrade. Be sure to state why the buyer should choose you. Are you a graduate student? Teacher of foreign languages? Or a professional translator? Make sure to state which languages you can translate, which file types you are capable of delivering (.txt, .doc, .docx, .html, .xml), and how long it will take you to deliver your work.

Gig extras: additional text, read the translated text and deliver in MP3 format, quick turnaround

Links: swechi calsolaroat nativechina

14) **Press Release**. Businesses use press releases to announce new products, services, or breaking news to the

media. To be effective a press release must be well written, newsworthy, and tell reporters why they need to tell your story. If you are an experienced journalist, or just have a knack for telling a compelling story, you may be able to write effective press releases. Be sure to highlight any marketing and writing experience in your gig description. Gig extras: add hyperlinked keywords for SEO optimization, added formatting options such as bullet points, headers, and logos, additional words, quicker turnaround, submit press releases to a certain number of websites

Links: ascottinc ricoramiro icematikx

Puppets

Believe it or not, Fiverr's biggest celebrity to date is none other than Professor Puppet, better known to his followers Professor Hans Von Puppet. In just over a year Professor Puppet has collected well over 2000 gigs. I've seen him featured in crowd funding campaigns, product testimonials, birthday greetings, and more.

The fact is - Professor Puppet has made two promotional videos for me. You can check them out on YouTube.

There's something about puppets that make them an ideal messenger to deliver business testimonials, commercial advertisements, birthday greetings and more.

The key to success here is going to be creating a totally unique character – redneck, hillbilly, celebrity (maybe a Dick Nixon, Barrack Obama, or Hillary Clinton, perhaps even a philandering Bill Clinton). If you can develop some kind of spin for your character, and put up three or four sample videos you will be off to a good start in puppet land.

Here is a look at several of the puppet celebrities on Fiverr and the gigs they are offering.

15) **Professor Puppet**. This guy would rank as "King" of the puppet acts. He's funny, convincing, and he's got a really good accent. Professor Puppet does a great job of interpreting your script, adding emphasis to key words, and

will even write / re-write your script if you need some help. He has a lot of great sample videos posted, and I can tell you from experience, he's great at getting gig extras. Each of the videos I had made was $20.00 to $25.00, but what would you expect from a "celebrity" who has a $100.00 offer for his "tip jar." If puppets are your thing, you need to check out Professor Puppet.

Gig extras: additional words, superimpose URL on screen, superimpose a different background, deliver your video in HD, deliver your video in one day

Link: professorpuppet

16) ***Dr. Puppet, West Coast Rap Star***. This guy will puppet your message or testimonial, or for an additional fee he can provide a great rap video that will really drive your message home. Another character offered, is Hillbilly Bob, the King of the South.

Gig extras: double length of video, rap the song that you provide, write lyrics and rap a song for your video, deliver video in one day

Link: puppets

17) **Harold the Puppet**. Harold is this crazy looking green puppet with an orange nose and nerdy glasses, sort of scary in a way. He will sing "Happy Birthday" or deliver a talk on anything you want. This one has a great gig description. It's well written, articulate and does a good job upselling the gig extras.

Gig extras: write or polish script, overlay logo or URL on screen, use custom background, deliver video in HD, deliver video in one day

Link: <u>puppetgrams</u>

Graphics and Design

Fiverr is a powerhouse when it comes to outsourcing artwork for small business. Fiverr gives small businesses the ability to easily outsource many of their everyday business needs. A short list of the more popular business related gigs includes – logo design, web banners, Facebook timelines, business card designs, flyers, advertisements, postcards and more.

The key to your success here is to act professional. Your lead in picture in your gig description should be one of three things in order of preference: 1) a professional video describing the services you provide, 2) a high quality picture of yourself flashing a big smile, 3) your company logo.

Next you want to show samples of your work. The more samples you show, the better your chances of closing the sale. Often times, buyers will make note of the ones they like, and tell you they want theirs like this one, or that one, except – can you change … Hence the need to show as many examples of your previous work as possible. One other thing I've seen some sellers do is to post a link to their portfolio online. Don't do it. Your buyer is on Fiverr looking to buy right now! Don't make any more work for him than you have to.

Even though businesses are only dropping five dollars, they need to know that you are a professional who can deliver a quality product on time. Be sure you act the part.

One thing I've noticed, especially in the logo design field – many of these sellers have twenty to twenty-five gigs in their queue at any given time.

18) **Logo Design**. Logo design is a booming service on Fiverr. The good designers all have twenty or more gigs in their queue, and most of them have a six to eight day time frame for delivery. One of the top sellers I looked at logo_business currently has 156 items in his queue, despite the fact that he has an eighteen day delivery time frame. A competitor of his currently has 64 items in his queue. Key phrases in all of the descriptions include "professional graphics designer," "experienced logo designer," "Blank years of experience."
Gig extras: deliver in different formats, deliver logo with different color variations, quicker turnaround, unlimited revisions
Links: logo_business experthq adamjohnson

19) **Infographic Design**. These are those neat little charts you see in magazines, and scattered all over the web. Usually they have three to four facts, and a related illustration or graph. One guy who has been offering this service has collected 1650 gigs in just eleven months, and he currently has twenty items in his queue. To succeed in this gig you need to be creative, and have a flair for display. Before you start any project make sure you know what your client wants. What size of graphic do they need? Ask about colors, numbers, products, and if they have a particular look or feel in mind. Once again you want to display as

many samples of your work as possible. The more you show, the more chances you will have to get your clients creative juices flowing.

Gig extras: make it bigger with more points on it, provide an editable vector file, quicker turnaround, offer to research and discover details for infographic

Links: forfiverr baskin35 javagirl2012

20) **Business Cards**. Business cards offer a growth opportunity on Fiverr. There are no big players, just a whole lot of small fish swimming around in a big pond. With the right offer you might be able to jump in and build a good sized business. The key will be writing an effective gig description. Make it long, 250 to 350 words. Play up your experience, any graphic design background you might have, and show plenty of samples. Right now, all of the gig descriptions are short, and none of the players have any real portfolio to show potential customers.

Gig extras: psd file of business card, additional images, quicker turnaround, create a QR code

Links: callmefay gadjet blueheck

21) **Facebook Timeline**. It's the hottest website out there, so it only follows that Facebook design would be in demand. Business is good, but complaints appear commonplace. Most sellers have considerably more negative reviews here than for any other services I've looked at. What you need to do is write a detailed gig description of what you can and cannot do. Offer revisions (either included in the gig, or as a gig extra). Make your picture policy clear. Will you provide pictures, pull them

from their Facebook pages, or does your customer need to upload all of the pictures that you need.

Gig extras: Design similar to your Twitter, Google or website, deliver psd file for later updates,

Links: Adin770 eghaz_01 zorroman mohsinkhan

22) **Twitter Background**. Similar to the Facebook gig listed above, except this one is for Twitter. If you can help people and businesses brand themselves, there are thousands of customers waiting for you. Again, the key is plenty of samples of your previous work, and a detailed explanation of what you can and cannot do.

Gig extras: psd file for later updates, provide background images, provide design in various formats, add links to YouTube, LinkedIn, Facebook, and Google +, install background

Links: callmefay vaughnonmovies

23) **Brochures, Flyers, and Postcards**. Not everyone has gone digital. Many businesses still rely on print media. If you have the knack to design postcards, flyers, and brochures there is a strong market for those services on Fiverr. Several sellers have collected 300 or more gigs in less than a year. I've seen several sellers spell out a lot of the places you can use their work. Also, make sure that you out who provides the art, if you are delivering at 300 dpi or what, and format item will be delivered in.

Gig extras: design a two sided brochure, include psd file, convert file to pdf, create a QR code, quicker turnaround

Links: sriramdesigns mariadesign fiverrstar alynna

24) **Website Banners & Headers.** Face it every business out there has one or more websites. Most businesses that have a website struggle to keep up, because the budget doesn't allow them to hire an IT professional to keep it up-to-date. If you can provide website services such as banners and headers, you're going to get business. This is another one of those services where many sellers have over a thousand gigs completed, and twenty to thirty more gigs in their queue. Make sure customers provide you with all of the information that you need: website URL, size requirements of banner needed, wording wanted, and pictures. Let people know if you will provide any revisions. Gig extras: additional revisions, provide in a different format, quicker turnaround, animate banner content, add links, provide psd file for easy editing, upload banner to site

Links: design2thrive datint quixotic designhub

25) **Website Landing Page**. This is another thriving niche. One new entry gathered 26 gigs in just two weeks, and has another ten in his queue. You can offer to do a landing page, sales page, or squeeze page. Be sure to show examples of each in your samples. Outline any types of work you won't do – gambling, porn, dating, etc. Mobile land pages seem to be selling as well or better than standard pages. You should probably mention a mobile landing page in your gig, and add a separate gig for a mobile landing page.

Gig extras: upload page to server, add Facebook and Twitter button links, integrate an email capture form into the page

Links: <u>iwsdesign</u> <u>b3bold</u> <u>smartbizz</u> <u>stevemitch</u>

Website services

Any service related to computers can make you big bucks on Fiverr. Sellers are offering just about any kind of computer gig that you can imagine: programming, website advice, website design, banner advertising, Facebook and Twitter timeline design, and eBay and Amazon services.

The really successful sellers make a point of mentioning their web accomplishments early in their gig descriptions. You need to tell them exactly what you can do, how long you have been doing it, and who you have been doing it for. If you don't want to drop specific company names, talk industries.

Expert advice and recommendations on customer website is a brisk seller, and offers the opportunity for many high priced gig extras. Some sellers offering Facebook timelines have 40 or 50 orders in their queue. Wordpress design, installation, and training are also popular.

The key to making money here is to play up your professionalism, and to carefully choose your gig extras for your maximum profit potential.

26) **Website review**. Several sellers are striking gold by offering website advice. They will go through your website page by page and provide a critical review letting you know where you need improvement. Some of the areas covered will be how to improve conversions, design, structure, SEO, and links. Reports are offered in writing, or as a step by step video.

Gig Extras: SEO Optimization report, extended video audit, consultation via Skype

Links: Chicagoslim bertmartinez

27) **Wordpress Customization / Installation**. One seller has collected over 1210 gigs in the last year offering to customize your wordpress site. The fiverr is just for the price of entry. After you discuss the plugin or options you want, they will send you the exact details, pricing, and timeframe. What a great way to get leads! Other sellers I've investigated offer to help recover your lost password, install you wordpress site,

Gig Extras: price by services required outside of Fiverr, add pages and content, add plugins

Links: seo_by_pro spark4hope

28) Website Threats. This one is a hackers dream. Every day the news headlines break stories about major sits being hacked, and customer data being hijacked. This is where you can come in as a hero. Offer to check customer's websites for vulnerability, and possible security risks. One seller has collected 253 gigs doing this in just the past year.

Gig Extras: charge for extra threat checks,

Links: securzone

29) Android / Mobile Apps. The mobile web is growing and developing quickly, and programmers are getting rich from it. Several sellers have rung up over 1000 gigs by offering to create mobile websites or cell phone apps. Your offering can be as simple as a mobile landing page,

optimizing an existing website for mobile, or developing custom apps.

Gig extras: Setup app on Google Play, add logos and images to app, provide QR codes, publish app to I Store

Links: upgradeyourself ttzachii

Time to get started selling

Thanks again for reading my book. I hope you learned what you needed to about selling on Fiverr. Compared to many on line sites, they've made selling super easy.

As you can see everyday people, just like you and me, are having fun and making money selling on Fiverr. My suggestion would be to spend a few hours looking through the different gigs already being offered. Take time to make notes on what they are offering, the wording of the offers, and the keywords they are using.

When you are done take a few minutes to review your notes. Write down what you like or don't like about each gig.

After you are done taking notes, go through your notes again. This time think about what kind of a spin you can put on each of the gigs to make it different or unique to you.

Finally, decide which gig you want to try. Write out your gig description. Upload your pictures and videos. Get ready for orders.

I wish you the best of luck.

And, may I ask a personal favor? If you have found this guide helpful would you please consider leaving a review on Amazon. Like everything else, people are eager to find out how to do things, but are unsure where to turn for advice. Reviews good, or bad, help them decide whether a book is right for them or not.

Also available on Kindle by Nick Vulich

Are you wondering how you can make a few hundred bucks fast, without hitting the streets? Would you like to know how you can put $100 in your hands, whenever you're running a little short on funds? Would you like to have your own personal money machine?

This book can help you with all of these things.

What you are about to learn is how to make $100 everyday selling on eBay.

What I'm going to give you is a proven plan that you can follow over and over again, to make money now – and in the future, whenever you find yourself strapped for a little cash.

What's the secret to selling your item for the most money possible?

It's easy…

Freaking Idiots Guide to Eliminating Medical Debt

How you can legally reduce or eliminate medical debt without bankruptcy

Nick Vulich

A recent report from Harvard University says that 62% of all bankruptcies are a direct result of medical bills. There you are going on with your life, and next thing you know, you're in the hospital. Maybe it's emergency surgery, a heart attack, a car wreck, or even the c – word (cancer). The bills can be devastating. Even a simple out-patient procedure such as gall bladder surgery can run from $25,000 to $30,000. A visit to the emergency room can be as much as $4,000 to $5,000.

Even with insurance, the out of pocket expenses can be crushing. Most insurance policies today have a 10 to 30 per cent co-pay. In the case of the $30,000 gall bladder surgery you could be stuck paying $3,000 to $9,000 depending upon what your yearly spending limit is set up at.

Blame it on companies trying to save money and offering employees watered down insurance policies, or hospitals and doctors inflating prices, or whatever else you can think of.

The fact is medical bill are a burden on everyone.

Coming Soon by Nick Vulich

Take your eBay sales to the next level.

In this book Nick guides you through the maze that is eBay stores. Learn how to open an eBay store, how to set up and optimize your store front, and how to put your best foot forward to eBay buyers.

Learn how to develop a pricing strategy for your store. Start planning sales to grow you store through a planned campaign employing Markdown Manager and Custom e-mails.

Here is a quick look at the Table of Contents.

Good luck, and great selling.

If you are happy with the information in this book, please visit the books page on Amazon, and leave a review. Your honest advice will be appreciated by all potential readers. As with anything, the more good reviews, the more people will be interested in looking at the book.

If you have any comments or questions, you can contact me at nick@digitalhistoryproject.com.

www.ingramcontent.com/pod-product-compliance
Lightning Source LLC
Chambersburg PA
CBHW071726170526
45165CB00005B/2172